LIFE ON A BARGE

a sketchbook

My Sources

Le Musée d' Intérêt National de la Batellerie,
Conflans-Sainte-Honorine, (Yvelines), France

The Science Museum, London

Office National de Navigation, Paris

Encyclopaedia Britannica

La Batellerie et Conflans-Sainte-Honorine
by François Beaudouin

The Erie Canal
by Peter Spier

Ships
by Björn Landström

Voies d' Eau et Bateliers du Nord,
by the Centre National de Documentation Pédagogique
and the Centre Régional de Documentation Pédagogique de Lille, France

...and my thanks

to Mr. and Mrs. Piet Van Wynen,
as well as to Mr. Paul Brinkman,
for my trip on a barge

to Mr. Ludovic de Noue, and to the entire crew of the pusher Valois
of the Compagnie Générale des Pousseurs
sur les voies navigables (CGPVN), in Paris

to Mr. Michel Zeller,
Mr. Charly Godefroy,
and Mr. Martial Chantre.

First published 1981 by Librairie Ernest Flammarion, Paris. Original title VOYAGE EN PÉNICHE © Flammarion 1981
English text copyright © 1982 by Huck Scarry. First American edition published 1982 by Prentice-Hall, Inc.

10 9 8 7 6 5 4 3 2 1

Library of Congress Cataloging in Publication Data : Scarry, Huck. Life on a barge. Translation of: Voyage en péniche.
SUMMARY: Discusses the canals found around the world, the barges which use them, and the people who operate these boats.
1. Canals—Juvenile literature. 2. Canal-boats—Juvenile literature. [1. Canals. 2. Boats and boating] I. Title.
TC745.S313   386' .4   81-20976   ISBN 0-13-535831-0   AACR2   ISBN 0-13-535824-8 (pbk.)

LIFE ON A BARGE
a sketchbook

by Huck Scarry

PRENTICE-HALL, INC.
Englewood Cliffs, New Jersey

This book is based on a real trip I took aboard
a barge in Holland. I became fascinated
by the life of barge-people, and my curiosity spurred me on
to learn more about barges and their past.
In addition to the journal of my trip, I have included
drawings of barges from several other countries.
I hope you enjoy this trip, and this book, as much as I did!

*West Church Tower,
built in 1631*

*Montelbaan Tower,
once part of the city walls,
built about 1485*

*The Mint Tower,
built about 1485*

In Holland

Recently, I had the opportunity
to take a trip on a barge.
I went to the city of
Amsterdam, in Holland, where
I was to meet the barge
on its journey.
Amsterdam is a lovely city,
crowned by many tall,
slender towers.
I had time to draw some of
the most beautiful ones.

South Church Tower,
built in 1614

The small "Weepers' Tower,"
built in 1482,
where wives said farewell
to their seafaring husbands

The "Old Church,"
built in the
thirteenth century

The city of Amsterdam

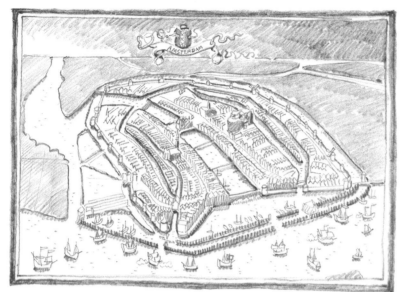

A bird's-eye view of Amsterdam in 1538,
drawn from a painting by Cornelius Antonisz
in the Amsterdam Historical Museum

Most cities
are built along busy avenues,
but the city of Amsterdam
is built around rings
of quiet, graceful canals.
Instead of cars and
trucks, you're likely to
see boats, swans, and ducks
in front of your house.
At a crossroad,
in place of a stoplight
you might find a
beautiful drawbridge.

Two of more than 800 bridges in central Amsterdam

Every year, about 50 cars take an accidental dip into the canals!

Herengracht

In winter, when they freeze, the canals make for fine skating.

Amsterdam Harbor

*A view of Amsterdam Harbor in 1686,
drawn from a painting
by Willem Van de Velde the Younger*

*The Royal Palace in the center of the city was once the
Town Hall. Built in 1655, this impressive edifice
gives an idea of Amsterdam's importance
in former times.*

*With sharp eyes, you can see a
sailing ship riding proudly
above the rooftops!*

In the seventeenth century,
Amsterdam was one of the most important ports in the world.
From here, daring captains searched for
a Northwest Passage to the Orient.
From here, the first trading vessels rounded the Cape of Good Hope
on their way to the Far East,
returning with the riches of distant lands.
Today, Amsterdam's harbor is still very busy,
though it is overshadowed by another
Dutch port (Europe's largest),
that of Rotterdam.

When I arrived, the boat I was about to board
was being loaded with sugar beets.
These beets were headed for a sugar refinery
where they'd be processed
to make sugar.

*(I have had to shorten the long barge
to get it all on this page!)*

The captain and his wife,
Mr. and Mrs. Van Wynen,
came to meet me
on the dock.
My skipper took my bag,
helped me aboard,
and showed me downstairs
to my cabin.

"As soon as the boat is loaded,
we'll be on our way!"
said the captain.

The root of the sugar beet
is the source
of much of the world's sugar.
Unlike sugar cane,
it can be grown in cool climates,
like that of Holland.
In 1811 after the British
blockaded sugar imports to France
from the West Indies,
Napoleon ordered the people to plant
sugar beets all over Europe.

*Shipbuilder's
plaque*

*Mr. Van Wynen's boat
is named after another skipper—
Mr. Van Wynen's father,
Adrian Jacopus.*

The Adja is a typical modern Dutch barge:
Tonnage: 750 metric tons (826 U.S. tons)   Length: 65 meters (213.3 feet)   Horsepower: 520
Draft: 2.45 meters (8 feet)   Width: 7.13 meters (23.4 feet)   Year built: 1962

At home aboard ship

Downstairs,
I had a chance to admire
the Van Wynens'
floating home.
It was spacious
and very neat.
While we waited
for the beets to be
loaded on board,
Mrs. Van Wynen
prepared some coffee,
and the Captain
took a moment to
catch up on
the latest news.

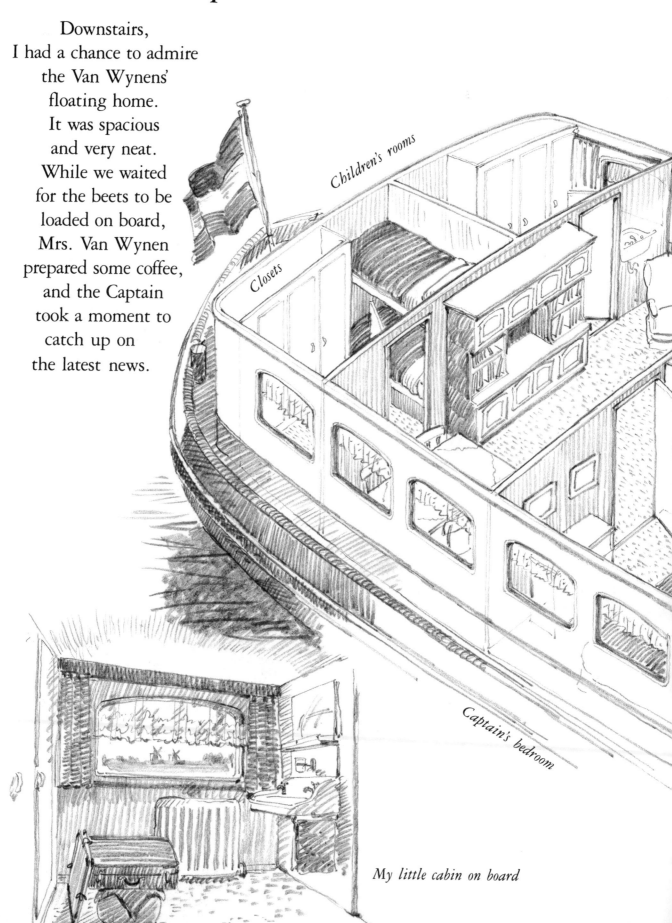

Children's rooms

Closets

Captain's bedroom

My little cabin on board

14

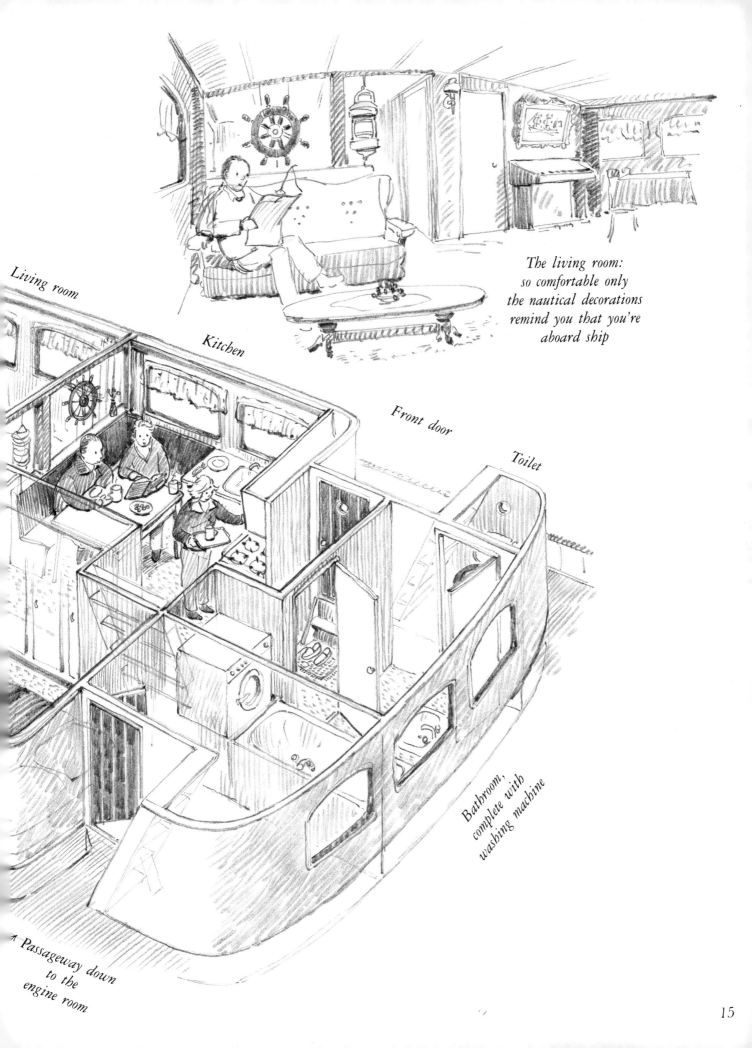

The living room:
so comfortable only
the nautical decorations
remind you that you're
aboard ship

Living room

Kitchen

Front door

Toilet

Bathroom,
complete with
washing machine

Passageway down
to the
engine room

15

In the wheelhouse

By far the most important room
in Captain Van Wynen's house
is the wheelhouse.
From here he guides his barge
along canals as well as rivers.

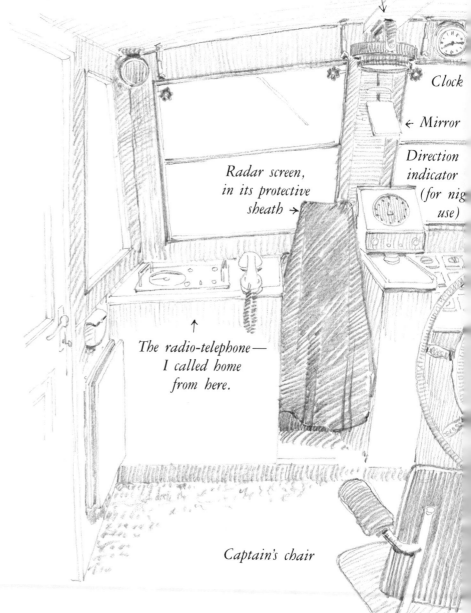

The compass is
placed upside down
on the ceiling,
where it is well away
from other
metal instruments.

Clock

← Mirror

Direction
indicator
(for nig
use)

Radar screen,
in its protective
sheath →

↑
The radio-telephone—
I called home
from here.

Captain's chair

No dirty shoes allowed
beyond the doormat!

All the captain's savings go into his barge.
Whenever he can, he buys better and newer equipment,
to keep everything up-to-date.

16

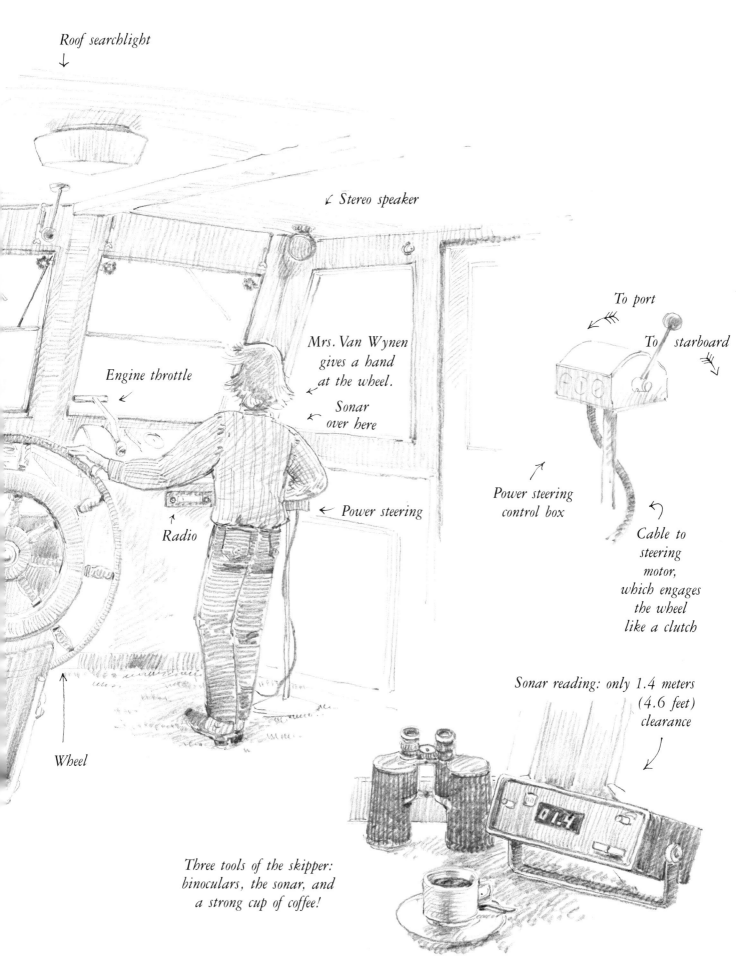

Roof searchlight
↓

↙ Stereo speaker

To port
↙

To starboard
↘

Engine throttle
↙

Mrs. Van Wynen gives a hand at the wheel.

Sonar over here ←

↑ Radio

Power steering control box

Power steering ←

Cable to steering motor, which engages the wheel like a clutch ↙

Wheel
↑

Sonar reading: only 1.4 meters (4.6 feet) clearance ↘

Three tools of the skipper: binoculars, the sonar, and a strong cup of coffee!

Archimedes' Principle

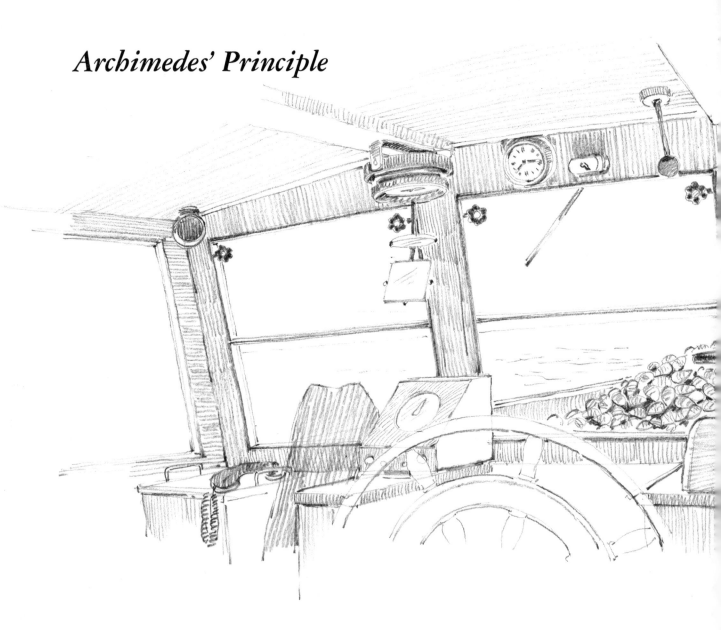

As more and more beets
were dumped into the hold,
the barge sank deeper
into the water.
Soon water lapped right
over the deck!
How could such a heavy boat
still stay afloat, I wondered.
The skipper gave me
a little demonstration
to explain
what is known as
Archimedes' Principle.

He took a pan of water, a tin cup,
and some coins.

The view from the helm:
beets as far as the eye can see!

The empty cup floated high
on the surface. Filling the
cup with coins made it sink a
bit, and at the same time the water
level rose. The weighted cup exerted a force equal to
the weight of the water it *displaced,* and
the water's pressure against the cup kept it afloat.

When the lesson was over...

In Holland, a land reclaimed from the sea,
there is a department of the government
called the Water Ministry.
This "Waterstaat" looks after dikes,
drainage of polders (reclaimed lowlands),
and depth of waterways.

. . . we were on our way!

Here is one of its boats on patrol.

You never stop waving aboard ship! Passers-by on ship and shore all return a wave and a smile.

Navigating

Just like drivers on the road,
skippers need signs
and signals
to guide their ships safely.
Here is a sampling
of the most frequent ones
I saw.

*"I'm passing on
the right."*

*Like automobiles, ships on waterways
pass on one another's left.
However, the ship going upstream
can decide to pass
on the right, if necessary.
He puts out a blue shield
to convey his intentions
and uses a blinking light at night.*

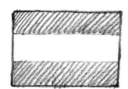

| Keep Right | No Anchoring | Whistle! | Speed Limit 6 kph (3.7 mph) | No Entry | Stay Between These Markers | No Parking |

Red

Red buoy

Channel

*River entry sign
for the River IJssel—
it looks just like the signs
on a highway.*

Green

*Black buoy
with white light*

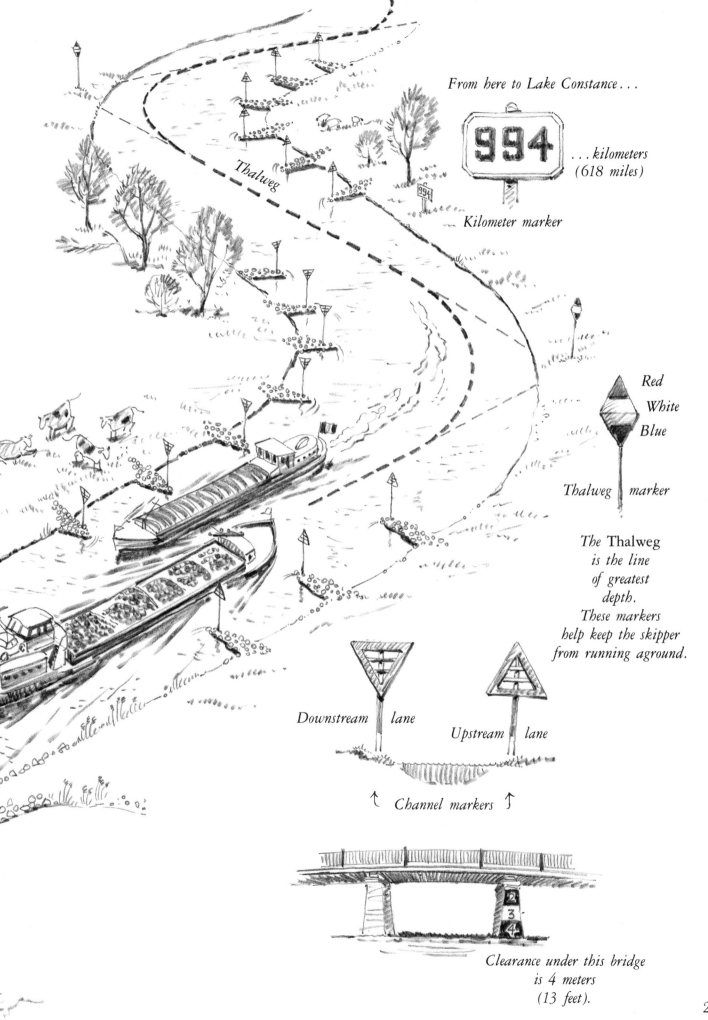

Thalweg

From here to Lake Constance...

994

...kilometers (618 miles)

Kilometer marker

Red
White
Blue

Thalweg marker

The Thalweg is the line of greatest depth. These markers help keep the skipper from running aground.

Downstream lane

Upstream lane

↑ *Channel markers* ↑

Clearance under this bridge is 4 meters (13 feet).

The Rhine

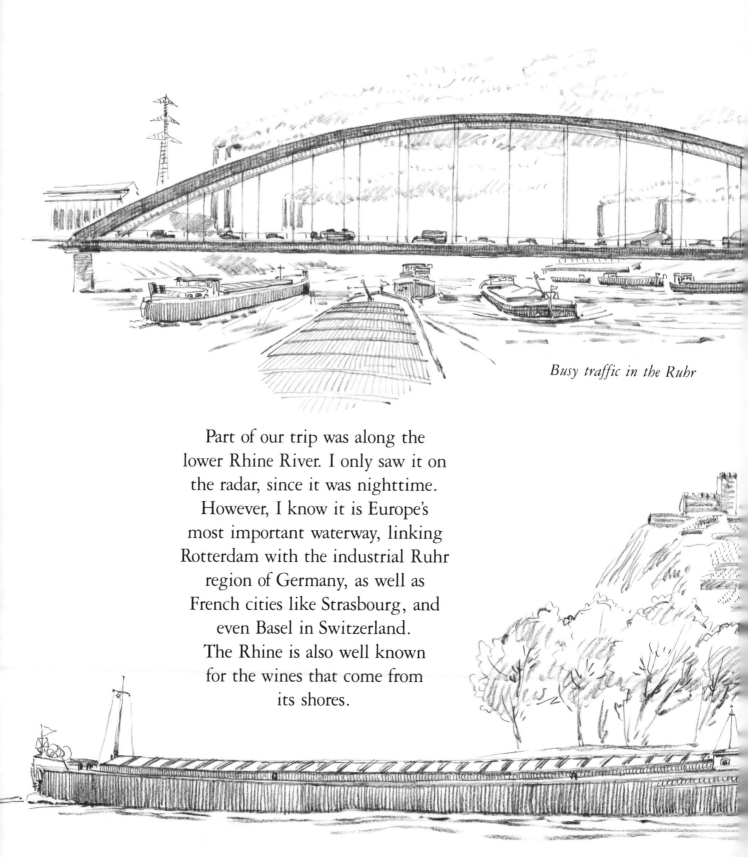

Busy traffic in the Ruhr

Part of our trip was along the
lower Rhine River. I only saw it on
the radar, since it was nighttime.
However, I know it is Europe's
most important waterway, linking
Rotterdam with the industrial Ruhr
region of Germany, as well as
French cities like Strasbourg, and
even Basel in Switzerland.
The Rhine is also well known
for the wines that come from
its shores.

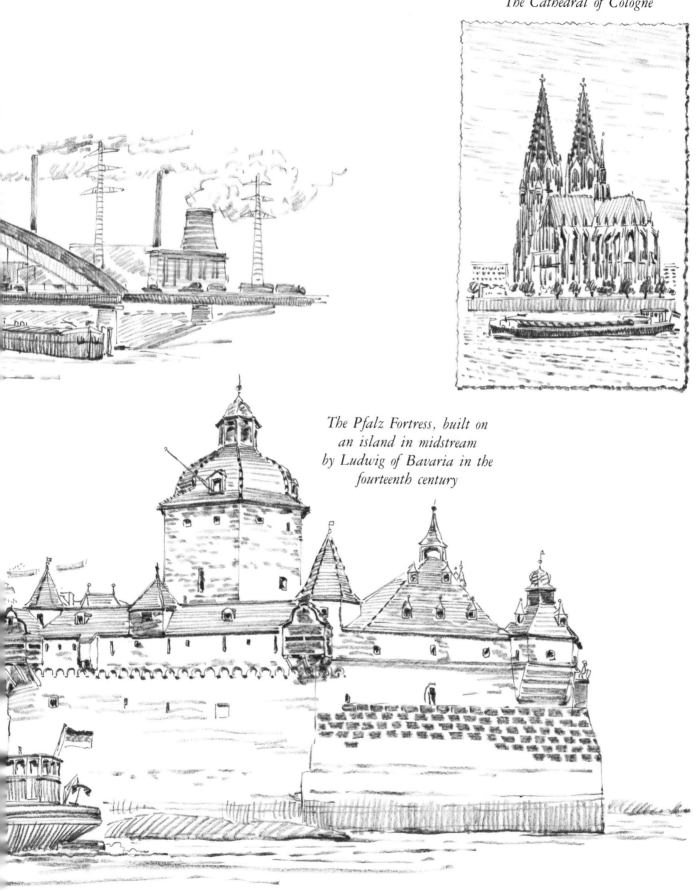

The Cathedral of Cologne

*The Pfalz Fortress, built on
an island in midstream
by Ludwig of Bavaria in the
fourteenth century*

25

*While her husband
snatches a bite to eat
belowstairs, Mrs. Van Wynen
takes the wheel.*

Sailing by night

When darkness fell, Mr. Van Wynen did
not tie up his ship for the night,
but continued on his way, navigating with the aid of radar.
During the sugar beet harvest, the Van Wynens' ship
works 24 hours a day, husband and wife taking turns
at the helm.
Time is money!

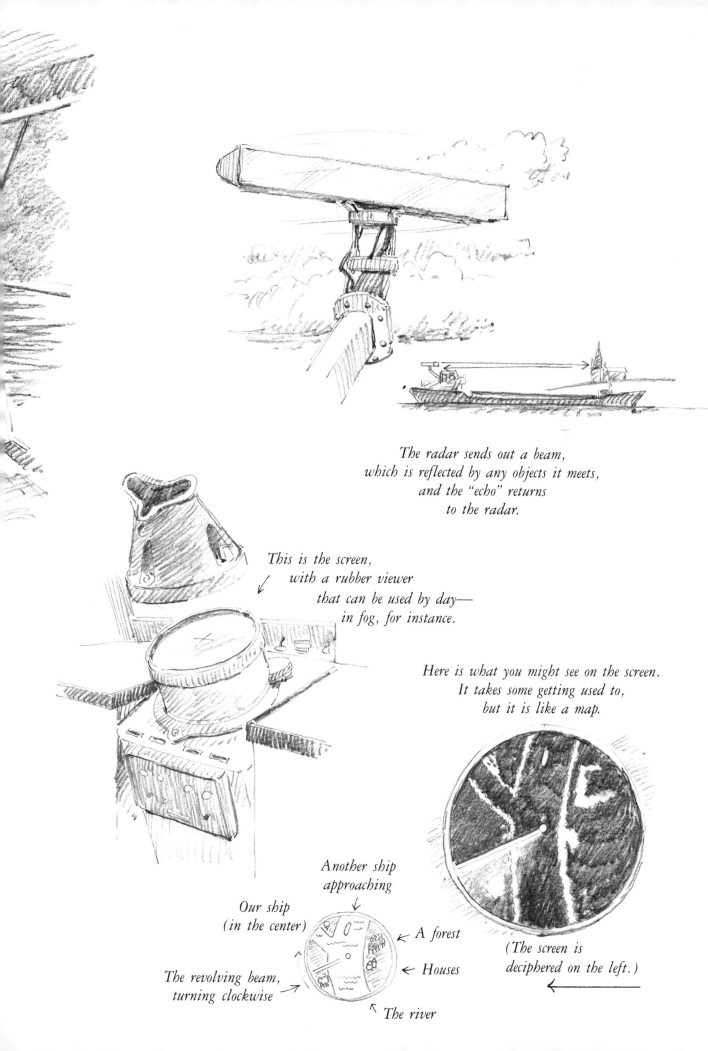

The radar sends out a beam,
which is reflected by any objects it meets,
and the "echo" returns
to the radar.

This is the screen,
with a rubber viewer
that can be used by day—
in fog, for instance.

Here is what you might see on the screen.
It takes some getting used to,
but it is like a map.

Another ship
approaching

Our ship
(in the center)

A forest

The revolving beam,
turning clockwise

Houses

(The screen is
deciphered on the left.)

The river

27

Early the next morning,
a small boat came alongside
to refuel the Van Wynens' barge with diesel fuel.
A barge as big as the Van Wynens'
needs a lot of power, and the engine
burns no less than 100 liters (26.5 gallons)
an hour.

*The small boat carries
all sorts of fuel
to keep the ship happy—
oil,
gasoline,
grease,
propane...*

*...and beer
for the captain!*

At our destination—the sugar refinery—huge cranes waited to unload the barge.
Swinging their huge shovels back and forth, they piled the beets
into mountains by the quay. What an impressive sight!

Finishing up

To pick up the last remaining beets in the hold,
a small bulldozer was lowered down by crane.
It artfully shuffled all the random beets
into a neat pile for the shovel.
Then the boat was given a good hosing down—
Mr. Van Wynen likes his house kept tidy!

The weekend

At the end of a busy week,
the Van Wynens need a rest.
They tie up the boat,
and with the aid of the small crane on board,
lower their car to the quay.

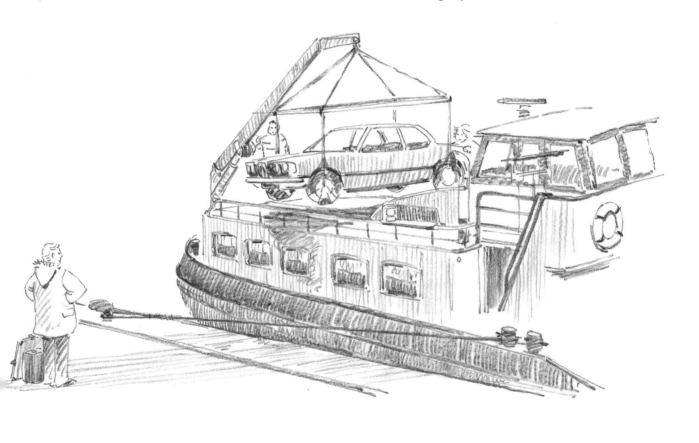

Bye! Bye!

In Belgium

Belgium, like Holland,
is a flat land
located near the mouth of the Rhine.
Waterway transport is as important here
as it is in Holland.
To accommodate the big modern barges
that travel the Rhine and the Lowlands,
the Belgians have widened and deepened
many of the major waterways.

*The Church
of the Holy Virgin
in Antwerp
overlooks the River Schelde
and one of the world's
busiest seaports.*

*One of the city gates in Tournus
bestrides the River Schelde
(also called the Escaut).*

Other canals are just big enough
to carry the traditional "Flemish barges"
that are still the principal type of barge
used in Belgium's neighbor, France.
Let's have a look...

In France

Unlike Holland and Belgium,
France is a country of diverse terrain.

The French built a canal system
using locks, so that boats could travel
throughout the country. Most canals in France
preserve the charm of the bygone days
in which they were built.
Indeed, France, unlike her neighbors
on the Rhine, hasn't modernized many
of her canals, and the barges you see
there today are the same ones
your great-grandfather could have seen.

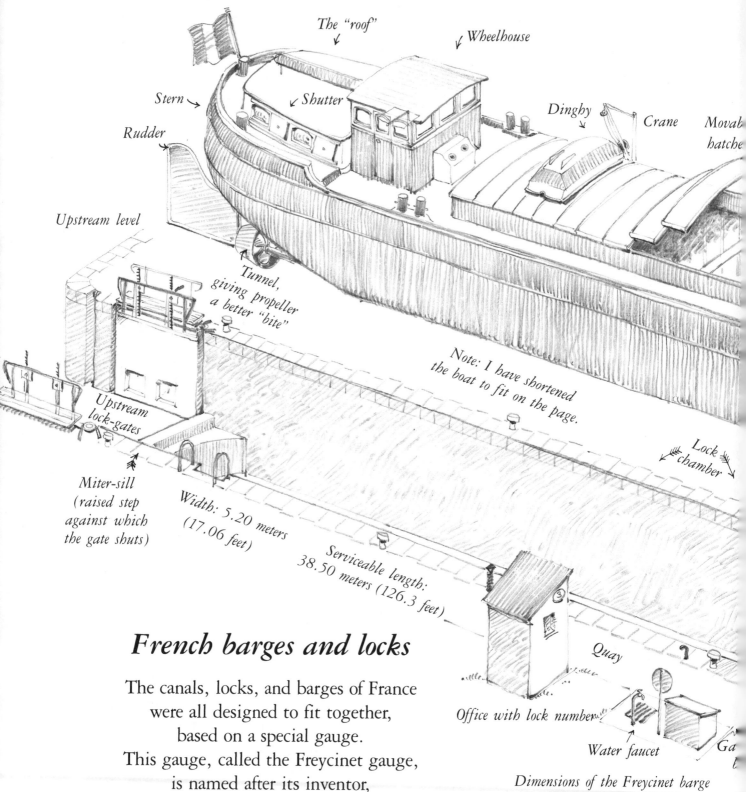

The "roof"

Wheelhouse

Stern

Shutter

Rudder

Dinghy

Crane

Movab
hatche

Upstream level

Tunnel, giving propeller a better "bite"

Note: I have shortened the boat to fit on the page.

Lock chamber

Upstream lock-gates

Miter-sill (raised step against which the gate shuts)

Width: 5.20 meters (17.06 feet)

Serviceable length: 38.50 meters (126.3 feet)

Office with lock number

Quay

Water faucet

Ga
l

French barges and locks

The canals, locks, and barges of France
were all designed to fit together,
based on a special gauge.
This gauge, called the Freycinet gauge,
is named after its inventor,
Charles de Freycinet,
minister of public works in 1878.
This gauge is based on the dimensions
of the Flemish barge,
the most popular of that time.

Dimensions of the Freycinet barge
Length: 38.50 meters
(126.3 feet)
Width: 5.06 meters
(16.6 feet)
Draft: 1.80 meters
(5.9 feet)
Tonnage: 240 metric tons
(264 U.S. tons)
Volume of the hold: 405 cubic meters
(1328.7 cubic feet)

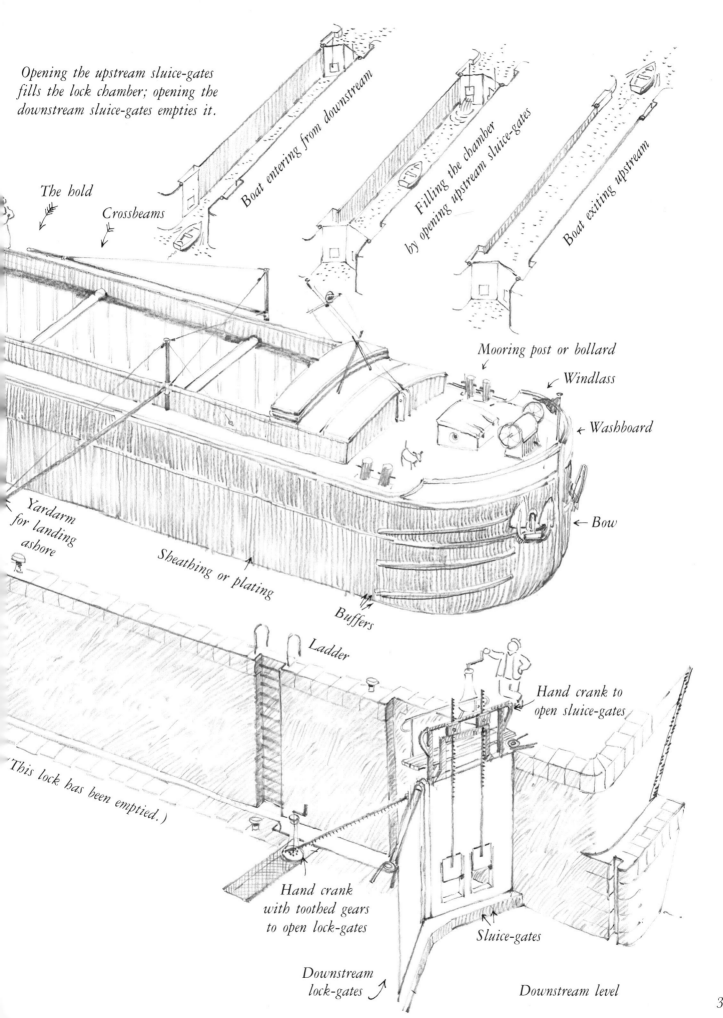

Opening the upstream sluice-gates fills the lock chamber; opening the downstream sluice-gates empties it.

Boat entering from downstream

Filling the chamber by opening upstream sluice-gates

Boat exiting upstream

The hold

Crossbeams

Mooring post or bollard

Windlass

Washboard

Yardarm for landing ashore

Bow

Sheathing or plating

Buffers

Ladder

Hand crank to open sluice-gates

(This lock has been emptied.)

Hand crank with toothed gears to open lock-gates

Sluice-gates

Downstream lock-gates

Downstream level

39

Navigable waterways
crisscross much of the French nation.

And there are surprising sights to be seen
hundreds of miles from the sea.

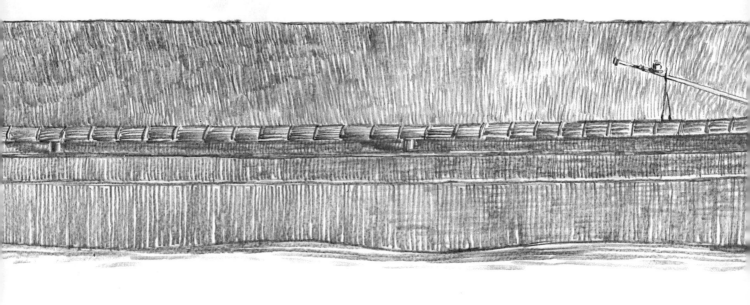

These remarkable canals take ships deep under hill . . .

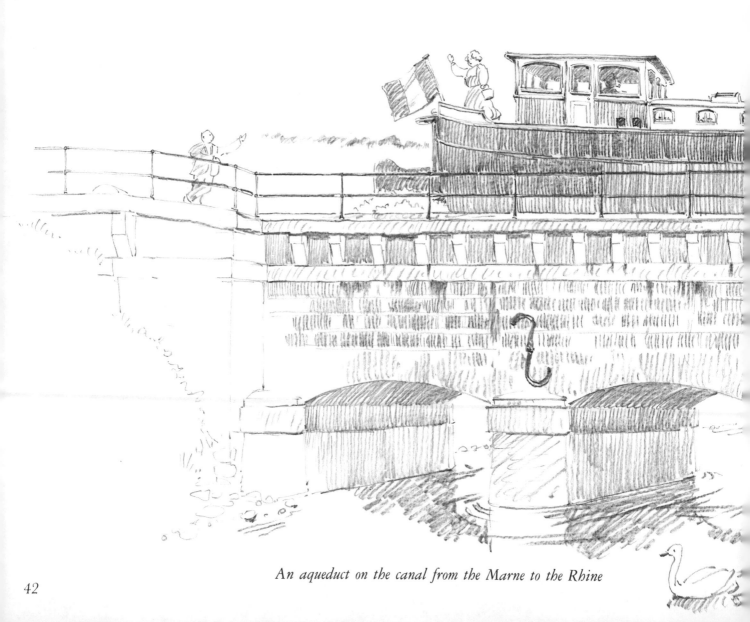

An aqueduct on the canal from the Marne to the Rhine

. . . and high over dale!

Life on board

Bargemen didn't always live aboard ship
with their families. Long ago, they lived on shore,
working their barges locally by day.
But then came the railway, bringing stiff competition
to the bargemen. To keep his customers,
the bargeman had to keep his prices low.
So he dispensed with his house and his crewmen
and brought his family to live on board and help him.

Inside a French barge

Most French barges are much smaller than Mr. Van Wynen's,

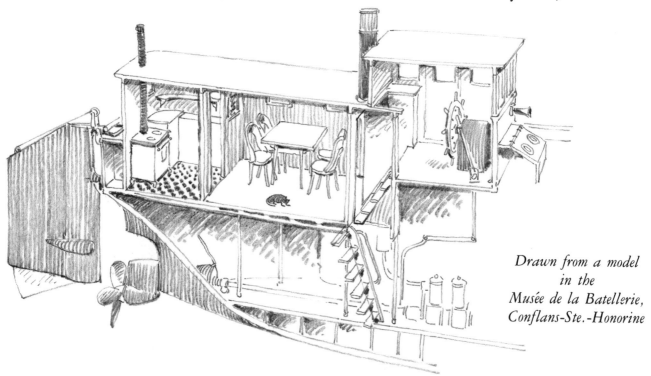

*Drawn from a model
in the
Musée de la Batellerie,
Conflans-Ste.-Honorine*

in order to travel the narrow canals.

In the living room

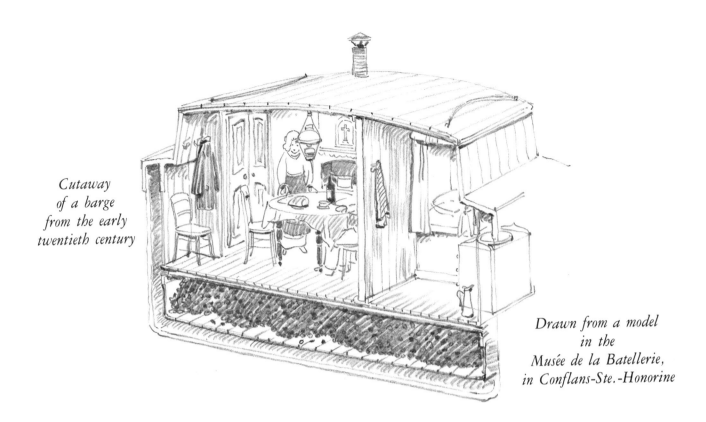

*Cutaway
of a barge
from the early
twentieth century*

*Drawn from a model
in the
Musée de la Batellerie,
in Conflans-Ste.-Honorine*

Before barges had their own engines,
they had to be hauled along from the shore
by horses and sometimes men.

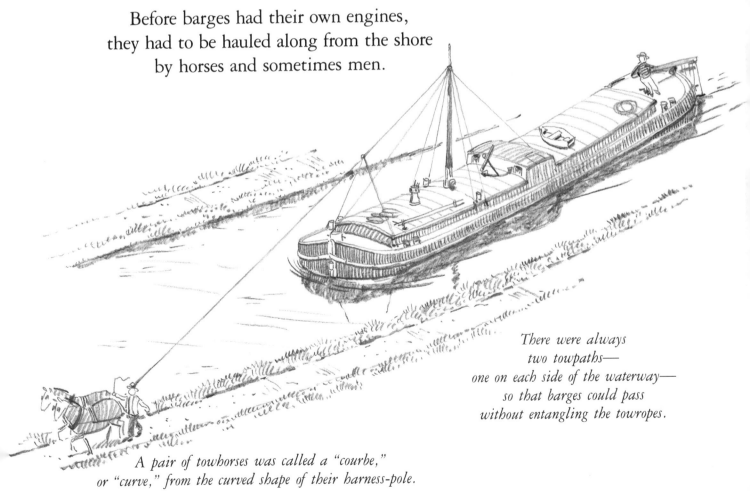

*There were always
two towpaths—
one on each side of the waterway—
so that barges could pass
without entangling the towropes.*

*A pair of towhorses was called a "courbe,"
or "curve," from the curved shape of their harness-pole.*

In the last century when skippers
brought their families on board to live,
it was impossible for children to
go to school, for they were
always traveling.

Unable to learn other trades, boat-children
knew only what they had learned aboard
ship, and inevitably they became skippers themselves
when they grew up. Mr. Van Wynen, for instance,
is the son of a skipper, of a skipper, of a skipper!
Today, all children must attend elementary school;
for boat-children, it means going
to special boarding school at the age of six.
Children and parents can only get together
on occasional weekends and holidays. Even today,
most boat-children leave school early,
to return to the family barge and help their parents
navigate. A boating son can eventually buy
his father's barge, and the retired captain
and his wife are able to live ashore—
but never too far from the sight of water!

Whoever has owned a boat
knows that the work
is never done.

A boat always needs washing...
repainting...
and numerous odd
repairs below deck
to keep her shipshape!

In the engine room

How the bargeman finds his work

Accompanying each shipment
is a way-bill (*lettre de voiture*).
Once the skipper delivers
a shipment, the recipient signs
the way-bill, with the date and hour.

A way-bill

With this document in hand,
the skipper presents himself to the
nearest Labor Exchange
(*La Bourse du Travail*).
Here, based on the
date of his last shipment,
the skipper receives a number
and is invited to attend
the next session of the Exchange.

At the same time, freight brokers
inform the Exchange of
the various shipments to be made.

NORD REGIONAUX · BASSE SEINE EXPORTATION

At the Labor Exchange

Boards indicating the
shipments to be made

Announcer

The skipper chooses his shipment.

How a shipment is listed on the board:

O 58	Pontaise	Rouen	blé	294ᵀ	18.73	22 après 12ᴴ	Sanara

A red light comes on ↘   *Loading*   *Unloading*   *Cargo*   *Weight*   *Freight*   *Loading*   *Freight broker*
when the shipment is chosen.   *port*   *port*   *number*   *time*   *to contact*

Once or twice a week the Exchange has a session.
The shipments offered to the skippers are posted on a board.
The skippers are called out by their numbers.
When his turn comes, a skipper chooses the
shipment he would most like to have.
The chosen shipment is marked by a red light.
Once the session is over, the skippers
contact the freight brokers, settle a contract,
and start off on a new journey.

The clock has just struck noon.
The lock is closed for lunch. Luckily there
is a village nearby. There's just enough time
for mother to fetch some groceries.

The children take out the garbage
and fill up the water tank.
Meanwhile, the captain
looks out for himself!

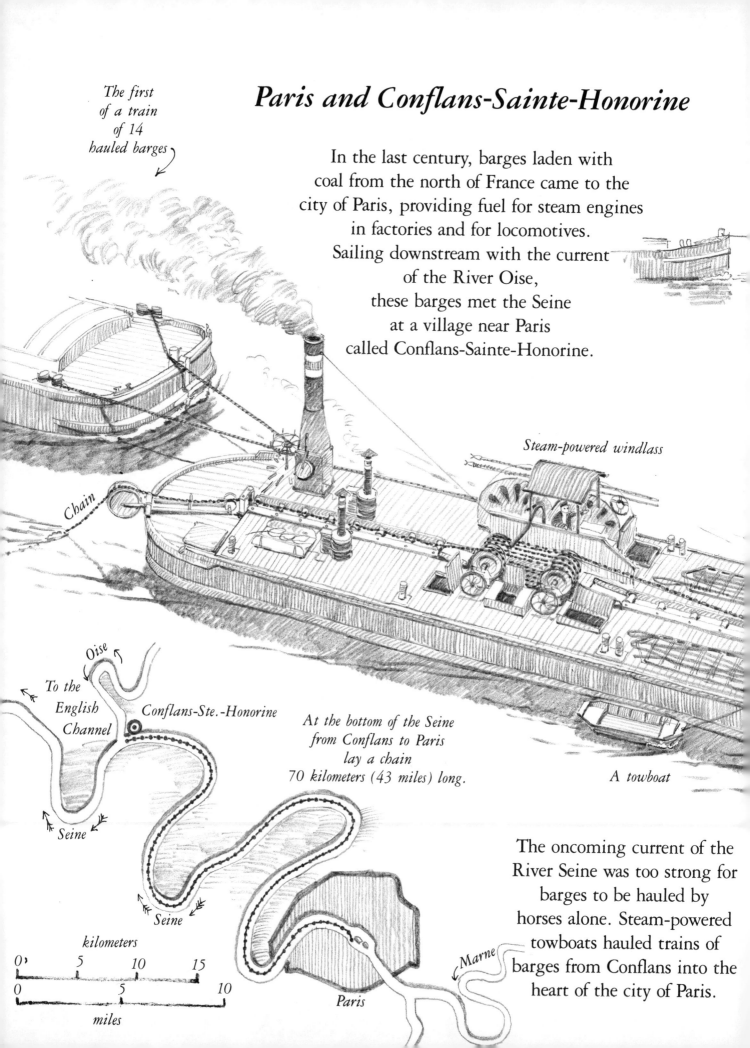

The first of a train of 14 hauled barges

Paris and Conflans-Sainte-Honorine

In the last century, barges laden with coal from the north of France came to the city of Paris, providing fuel for steam engines in factories and for locomotives. Sailing downstream with the current of the River Oise, these barges met the Seine at a village near Paris called Conflans-Sainte-Honorine.

Steam-powered windlass

Chain

Oise

To the English Channel

Conflans-Ste.-Honorine

At the bottom of the Seine from Conflans to Paris lay a chain 70 kilometers (43 miles) long.

A towboat

Seine

Seine

Marne

Paris

kilometers

0   5   10   15

0   5   10

miles

The oncoming current of the River Seine was too strong for barges to be hauled by horses alone. Steam-powered towboats hauled trains of barges from Conflans into the heart of the city of Paris.

The smokestacks could be folded down to pass beneath bridges.

A tugboat negotiating a bridge

These towboats had neither paddle wheels nor propellers, but hauled themselves along on a sturdy chain sunk on the riverbed. Although extremely powerful, a towboat was nonetheless limited by the length of its chain. The towboats were gradually replaced by tugboats until barges were provided with engines of their own.

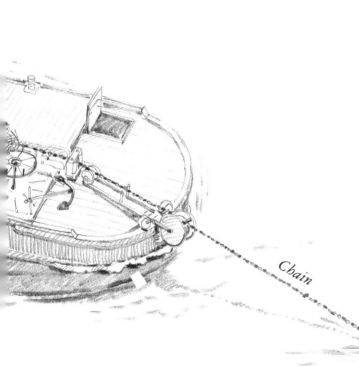

Chain

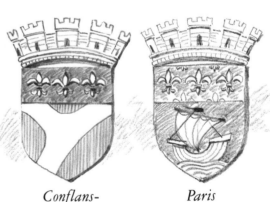

Conflans-Ste.-Honorine

Paris

The coats of arms of both cities pay tribute to the River Seine, on whose banks they grew. That of Conflans shows the meeting place of the rivers Seine and Oise. That of Paris shows a ship on the waves, although this city, by water, lies more than 360 kilometers (225 miles) from the sea!

A city of boats . . . Paris!

The old port of Paris

From an engraving in the Musée de la Batellerie, Conflans-Ste.-Honorine

Well before the age of steam,
the waterways of Paris bustled with activity.
Wood, used as a fuel
as well as for building, was floated
downstream to the capital on boats.

The Ile Louvier in 1736, from an engraving in the Musée de la Batellerie

In Paris, the wood was dried and
stored on an island in the Seine,
the Ile Louvier, which has since
been joined to the city's right bank.

Another flourishing activity in Paris was the arrival
and departure of packet-boats,
or *coches d'eau*. These boats carried passengers
to and from the capital on the Seine.
Resting overnight in riverside hostelries
along the way, one could travel
through much of France this way.

A French packet-boat, or coche d'eau.

59

British waterways

The Barton Aqueduct on the Duke of Bridgewater's canal, 1761

The first canal in Britain was built
by the Duke of Bridgewater in 1761, to transport coal
from his mines to the city of Manchester.
Designed by James Brindley, this canal
even had a tunnel and an aqueduct.
The novel idea made the duke's coal
less expensive and was an immediate success.

Sluice-gate crank

JULIET

K. HOLLINSHEAD
BIRMINGHAM

The duke's canal inspired a fever of canal building
throughout Britain, linking the major cities.
However, the canal system was short-lived, for the
newly designed railways soon transported goods much faster.

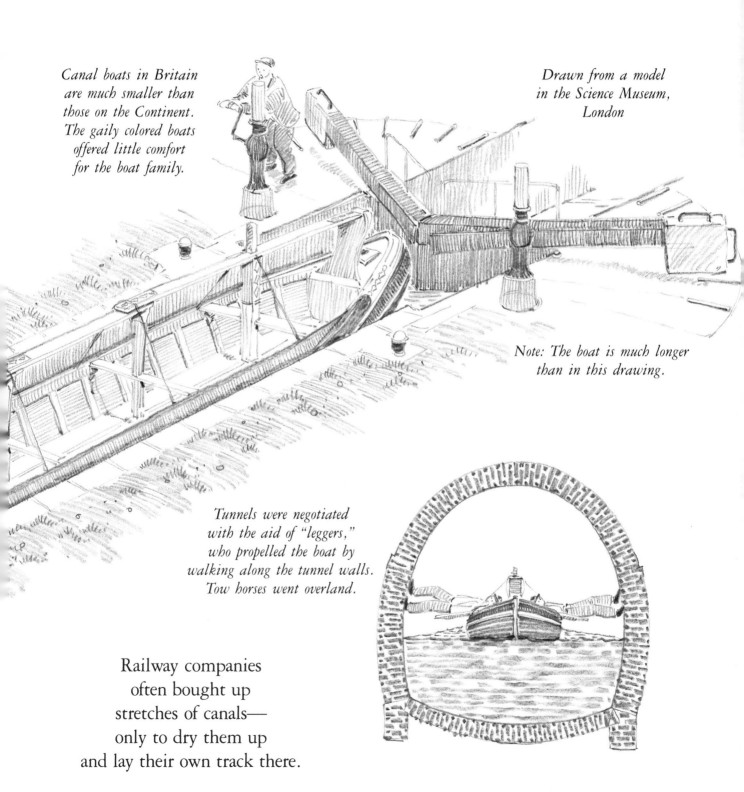

*Canal boats in Britain
are much smaller than
those on the Continent.
The gaily colored boats
offered little comfort
for the boat family.*

*Drawn from a model
in the Science Museum,
London*

*Note: The boat is much longer
than in this drawing.*

*Tunnels were negotiated
with the aid of "leggers,"
who propelled the boat by
walking along the tunnel walls.
Tow horses went overland.*

Railway companies
often bought up
stretches of canals—
only to dry them up
and lay their own track there.

*Erie Canal barges had
their own stables on board.*

The Erie Canal

The first long canal in the United States was the Erie Canal,
opened in 1825. It linked the Hudson River at Albany
with the city of Buffalo on the Great Lakes, thus making
a direct route by water from New York City to the distant
frontiers of the West. The canal allowed profitable transport
in both directions. Manufactured goods from the
East Coast were sent westward to the frontier towns,
and produce and grain came back from the farms, eastward to the
coastal cities. As in England, the canal carried not only freight
but also passengers, aboard comfortable packet-boats.

To pass,
the towline of one barge
was sunk beneath
the oncoming barge.

Although new railroads once stole a good part of its traffic,
the Erie Canal, improved and enlarged, still exists today,
forming part of the active New York State Barge Canal System.
The United States is also rich in large natural
waterways, like the Mississippi.
Here, powerful "pushers," like waterbound locomotives,
convey cargo throughout the center of the country.
The idea of using pushers spread to Europe, and I was
lucky enough to take a trip through Paris aboard one called the Valois.
Here is what I saw . . .

The future

A train of barges hauled by a tugboat,
or towboat, needed a crew to steer *each* barge
and keep it in line. However, a train
of *pushed* barges firmly tied together
can be handled as if it were
one long barge.

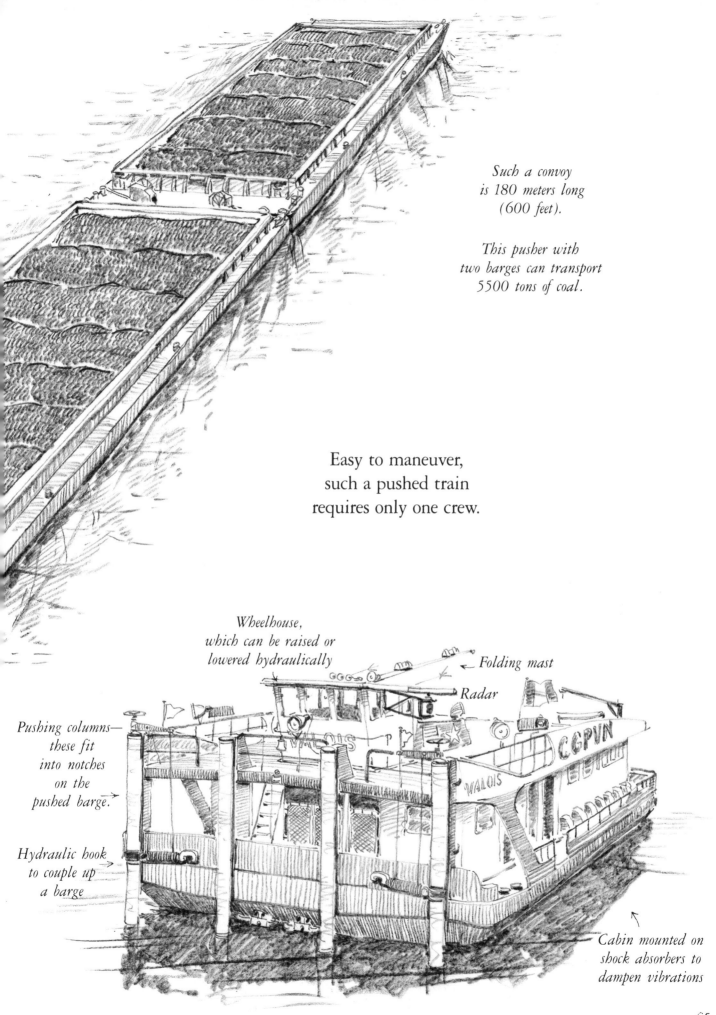

Such a convoy
is 180 meters long
(600 feet).

This pusher with
two barges can transport
5500 tons of coal.

Easy to maneuver,
such a pushed train
requires only one crew.

Wheelhouse,
which can be raised or
lowered hydraulically

← Folding mast

Radar

Pushing columns—
these fit
into notches
on the
pushed barge.→

Hydraulic hook
to couple up
a barge

Cabin mounted on
shock absorbers to
dampen vibrations

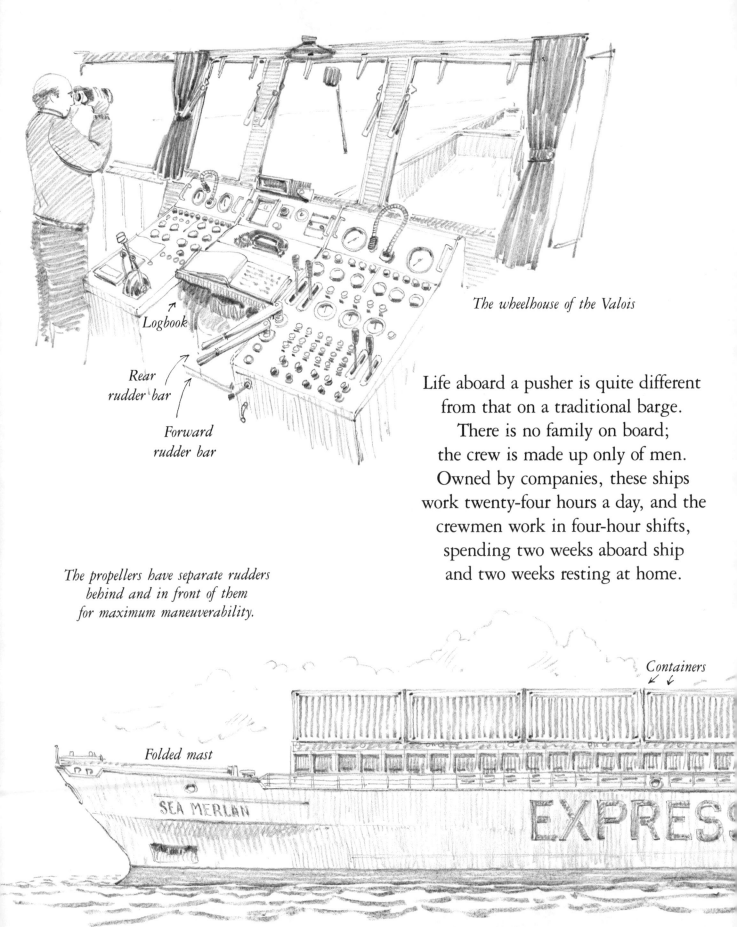

The wheelhouse of the Valois

Logbook

Rear rudder bar

Forward rudder bar

Life aboard a pusher is quite different
from that on a traditional barge.
There is no family on board;
the crew is made up only of men.
Owned by companies, these ships
work twenty-four hours a day, and the
crewmen work in four-hour shifts,
spending two weeks aboard ship
and two weeks resting at home.

*The propellers have separate rudders
behind and in front of them
for maximum maneuverability.*

Containers

Folded mast

SEA MERLAN

EXPRESS

A modern container ship I saw in Paris

The ship you see below is one
I was surprised to see in the center of Paris.
It is a container ship, able to sail the
high seas but small enough with its telescopic wheelhouse
to pass under bridges and go
through big locks. The containers, stacked
like blocks on board, can be lifted
by crane onto trucks or railway flatcars.
This versatile system
has a promising future, and is today's
expression of our most
ancient means of transport...

...by waterway!

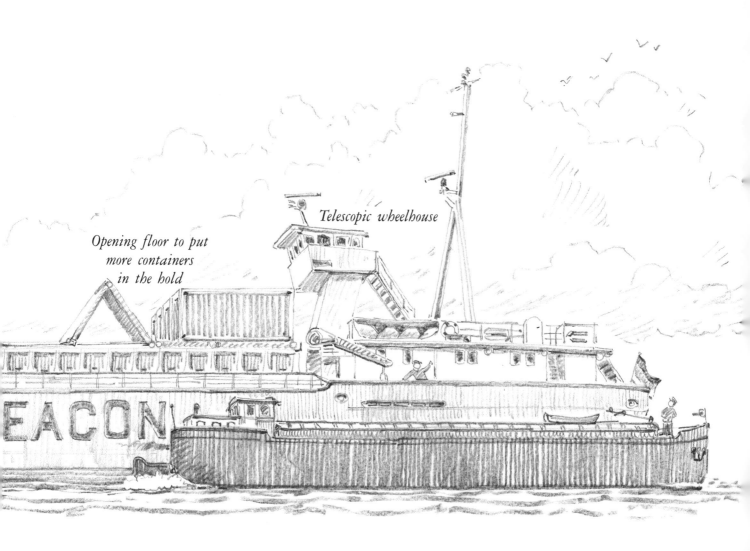

Telescopic wheelhouse

*Opening floor to put
more containers
in the hold*

Conclusion

Traveling on quiet canals, far from highways
and towns, can take one back to romantic times
when distances were measured in days and not minutes.
Indeed, barges are still allowed to travel at only
6 kilometers (3.7 miles) per hour on many canals, so as not to
destroy the canal banks with their wake!
Nevertheless, this mode of transport—too often forgotten—
is most economical, which should guarantee it an important
place in the future.

About the artist

*Huck Scarry, son of children's book author/illustrator
Richard Scarry, was born in Westport, Connecticut,
where he spent his childhood.
Later he moved to Switzerland with his parents.
He studied art in Lausanne, Switzerland, and now lives
in the old town of Geneva with his wife Marlis and their young daughter Fiona.
He has written and illustrated several other books for children,
including the popular* Steam Train Journey, On Wheels, *and* On the Road.

PUSHER WITH TWO BARGES

SEINE RIVER BARGE

RHÔNE RIVER BARGE

RHINE RIVER BARGE

"FLEMISH" BARGE

SOUTHERN FRENCH BARGE

ENGLISH CANAL BARGE